Extreme Biology

Hostile Homes

Extreme Habitats

Angela Royston

Gareth Stevens
PUBLISHING

Please visit our website, **www.garethstevens.com**. For a free color catalog of all our high-quality books, call toll free 1-800-542-2595 or fax 1-877-542-2596.

Library of Congress Cataloging-in-Publication Data

Royston, Angela, 1945- author.
 Hostile homes : extreme habitats / Angela Royston.
     pages cm. — (Extreme biology)
 ISBN 978-1-4824-2244-3 (pbk.)
 ISBN 978-1-4824-2245-0 (6 pack)
 ISBN 978-1-4824-2242-9 (library binding)
 1. Extreme environments—Juvenile literature. 2. Habitat (Ecology)—Juvenile literature.
 3. Adaptation (Biology)—Juvenile literature. I. Title.
 GE140.5.R69 2015
 577.58—dc23

2014027566

First Edition

Published in 2015 by
Gareth Stevens Publishing
111 East 14th Street, Suite 349
New York, NY 10003

© 2015 Gareth Stevens Publishing

Produced by: Calcium, www.calciumcreative.co.uk
Designed by: Paul Myerscough
Edited by: Sarah Eason and John Andrews
Picture research by: Rachel Blount

Photo credits: Cover: Shutterstock: David Krijgsman; Inside: Dreamstime: John Anderson 36, Andreanita 20, Betty Angleton-Halsey 15, Marcin Ciesielski/Sylwia Cisek 32, Ed Corey 41, Mircea Costina 39, Marconi Couto De Jesus 11, Anna Galejeva 38, Gemsbok 6, Inavanhateren 40, Stig Karlsson 19, Julie Lubick 30, Bruce Macqueen 3, 23, Mikael Males 31, Vivian Mcaleavey 7, Mikelane45 13, Pabkov 14, Pseudolongino 44, Qweszxcj 10, Salparadis 29, Darryn Schneider 1, 18, Vladimir Seliverstov 25, Nico Smit 12, Staphy 22, Mogens Trolle 24, Anke van Wyk 16, Robert Zehetmayer 43; NOAA: Lophelia II 2010 Expedition, NOAA-OER/BOEMRE 33, Dr. Ken Sulak, USGS/Life on the Edge 2004 Expedition: NOAA Office of Ocean Exploration 35, Edie Widder 34; Shutterstock: Solodov Alexey 37, Eric Broder Van Dyke 8, EastVillage Images 42, Erichon 4, P. Fabian 28, Carles Fortuny 26, Incredible Arctic 21, Jan Kaliciak 45, Sally Scott 17, Aleksey Stemmer 5, Paul Vinten 9, Alexander Yu. Zotov 27.

Printed in the United States of America

CPSIA compliance information: Batch #CW15GS: For further information contact Gareth Stevens, New York, New York at 1-800-542-2595.

Contents

Chapter 1

Colonizing Every Corner

Earth is the only place in the universe where we know for sure that life exists. Some parts of Earth are ideal for living things. Other parts are extremely difficult, and only exceptional plants, animals, and microorganisms, the smallest living things, can survive there.

No Place Like Home

Earth is divided into large areas, called biomes. Rain forests, deserts, and grasslands are all biomes. Each biome has a particular type of climate, which determines how easy or challenging it is for life to survive there. Millions of plants and animals live in hot, wet rain forests, but only a few species can live in deserts and on high mountaintops. Each biome consists of many different communities or habitats. The habitats provide the plants and animals with what they need to survive, particularly water, nutrients, warmth, and oxygen.

Africa's savanna is home to many animals, including antelope and zebras—and their predators.

Easy or Tough Living

Some habitats, such as coral reefs, support a lot of species of plants and animals, but other habitats are more specialized. Even favorable habitats can have hostile corners. Predators lurk around coral reefs, but clownfish stay safe by hiding among the stinging tentacles of sea anemones. A clownfish is immune to the stings—but its predators are not. In this book, we look at how plants and animals survive in some of the most extreme biomes and habitats on Earth.

The stinging tentacles of a sea anemone are hostile to most animals, but not to a clownfish.

Extreme!

Survival Superstars

Some living things manage to survive in places that are deadly to most other forms of life. These survival superstars are called extremophiles, and some can even live without oxygen! Most extremophiles are very small. In fact, they are so small you would need a microscope to see them.

Acid Attack

Acid bogs are some of the most hostile habitats. As well as being acidic, these wet and spongy areas have little or no nitrogen, an essential nutrient for plants to grow. However, any plant that manages to live there gains a huge advantage because it does not have to compete with other plants. Some plants have developed an amazing way of surviving in acid bogs—they feed on insects.

Catching Flies

In most habitats, animals rely on plants for food. Meat-eating, or carnivorous, plants have reversed this food chain. While most animals get nitrogen and other nutrients from plants, carnivorous plants get nitrogen by slowly breaking down and digesting insects and other small prey. A carnivorous plant can digest a small fly in a few hours, but may take several days to deal with something larger.

A fly cannot escape from the grip of a Venus flytrap.

Setting the Trap

Carnivorous plants have a strong, sweet smell, which attracts flies and other insects to them. Sundews have sticky leaves like flypaper. When a fly lands on a leaf, the leaf curls up, trapping the fly. The two leaves of a Venus flytrap snap shut when an insect lands on them. The pitcher plant has a different ploy. Its leaf forms a deep container filled with liquid. The sides are smooth and slippery, and lined with hairs that point downward. Once prey slide in, it is impossible for them to climb out. They fall into the liquid and drown.

Extra Extreme

A pitcher plant is big enough to collect a load of insects, especially in summer. By fall, the pitcher is packed with flies, moths, wasps, and other insects. It may capture a frog, a lizard, or even a mouse!

Salt Solutions

Living things need water, but not really salty water. Even most sea animals cannot survive in brine, which is water that is saltier than the sea. Yet some species do manage to live in extremely salty water. They can do so because they have smart ways of getting rid of extra salt.

Brine Shrimps

Salt lakes are so salty they are sometimes called "dead seas," but most salt lakes are able to support a few extraordinary forms of life. Brine shrimps thrive in the Great Salt Lake in Utah and Mono Lake in California. The shrimp's outer layer is waterproof and so it keeps out the salt. A brine shrimp feeds mainly on the larvae of brine flies. The shrimp's stomach lining absorbs the salt in the larvae and pumps it out through its gills.

Great Salt Lake is so salty that only extreme species can survive in its hostile waters.

Mangrove trees grow in salty soil along tropical coasts. Special roots grow upward to take in oxygen from the air.

Amazing Mangroves

Mangrove trees grow along seashores, where the sea covers the soil and the roots of the trees at high tide. The soil is really salty. Different types of mangrove trees have developed different ways of dealing with the problem. Some have special roots, like snorkels, which stick out of the mud to take in oxygen from the air. Others store surplus salt in their leaves. When the salt becomes too toxic, the leaves simply drop off.

Extreme!

Muddy Extremophile

The mud at the bottom of Mono Lake is especially hostile. It is incredibly salty, has no oxygen, and is extremely alkaline. Alkaline is the opposite of acidic, so the bacterium *Spirochaeta americana*, which lives in the lake, could definitely not survive in an acid bog. *Spirochaeta* only likes salty muds that stink of sulfur—like the smell of bad eggs!

Chapter 2

Hot Deserts

Deserts are the world's driest biomes, but not all deserts are the same. Some are sandy and have high sand dunes; others are stony. The most hostile deserts are not only dry but also scorching hot during the day and cold at night. Living there is very difficult and calls for some extreme solutions.

Hottest and Driest Deserts

The Sahara Desert in North Africa and the Mojave Desert in the Southwest United States are the world's hottest deserts. The highest temperature recorded was in Death Valley in the Mojave Desert in 1913, when the temperature reached 134°F (57°C). You might expect the hottest deserts to also be the driest—but they are not. The Atacama Desert on the west coast of South America is the driest desert, with some parts not having seen rain for more than 400 years! However, the average summer temperature there is only 65°F (19°C).

Death Valley usually gets less than 2 inches (5 cm) of rain a year. The mostly bare ground reveals the curious, folded shapes of the hills.

Extra Extreme

Parts of the Atacama Desert are too dry even for microorganisms to survive. Without microorganisms, nothing ever rots. The dry, dead leaves of plants that grew thousands of years ago still lie there on the ground!

Living in a Desert

Deserts look empty and barren, but some incredible species have adapted to live there, with little water and in fierce heat. Desert animals include gerbils, kangaroo rats, pocket mice, and other small mammals, as well as snakes, lizards, and many types of insects. Some desert birds, such as owls, nest in cacti, but most birds are only visitors. They fly into and out of the deserts, hunting for prey.

A flamingo feeds in a salt lake high in the mountains in the Atacama Desert.

Dealing with Heat

The lack of trees and other plants in deserts means that there are few places for animals to find shelter from the hot sun. Snakes and lizards often find some shade under large stones or bury themselves in the sand. Other desert animals get out of the scorching heat by burrowing below the surface.

Underground Homes

Although the desert surface may be deadly hot, just a few feet down the sand is cooler. Gerbils, kangaroo rats, gila monsters, sand cats, and foxes are just some of the desert animals that dig burrows. Gerbils and kangaroo rats eat seeds and other food they find in the soil but, like other desert animals, they also leave their burrows in search of something to eat. They wait until the temperature begins to fall before they venture up to the surface.

The Cape fox's big ears help it keep cool and hear prey underground.

Extra Protection

Even animals that shelter in burrows have extra adaptations to help them deal with the heat. Sand cats have thick fur on their paws to protect their feet on the hot ground. Desert foxes have extra-big ears, which let heat escape from inside their bodies and cool them down. Most desert animals are well camouflaged—they blend in with their surroundings, making it harder for predators and prey to see them.

Thick fur insulates an Arabian sand cat from the heat of the sun and keeps it warm at night.

Extreme!

Insect Sun Lovers

Saharan desert ants do not avoid the heat—they wait for the hottest time of day to hunt. Their long legs keep their bodies safely above the burning ground. The ants look for insects that have died in the heat. However, even these little daredevils can only stay in the sun for a few minutes at a time.

Living Without Water

Animals that live in deserts have to survive with little or no water. Many get all the water they need from the food they eat. Some, such as camels and monitor lizards, carry stores of fat in their bodies, which they break down into food and water.

Designed for Deserts

Camels are champions at surviving in the desert. Their humps contain so much fat they can last several weeks without eating and 7 to 10 days without drinking. When they reach water sources, they can gulp down 36 gallons (135 l) in less than 15 minutes! Camels have adapted to deserts in other ways, too. Their long, thin legs keep their bodies high above the hot ground, while their eyelashes and the hairs in their ears keep out sand blown in the wind.

A camel is at home in the desert. It can walk 100 miles (160 km) without water. It can even close its nostrils during a sandstorm to keep sand out.

No Sweat!

Most mammals lose water when they breathe out, when they eliminate their waste, and when they sweat. You sweat to cool yourself down when you are hot, so you might expect desert animals to be extra sweaty. However, the opposite is true. The bodies of most desert animals have adapted to keep water. Their feces are extremely dry, and their urine is so concentrated it contains very little water. Finally, they do not sweat. Kangaroo rats can even make water as they digest food, so they never need to drink.

Extra Extreme

Desert animals save water by having extra-strong urine. A camel's urine can be so strong it is as thick as syrup. It is not sweet like syrup though—it smells disgusting! In very extreme conditions, most of the urine turns into tiny, solid crystals.

How Do Desert Plants Survive?

Plants cannot survive without water, so large areas of deserts are bare. In many deserts, however, it can rain from time to time. When it does rain, desert flowers may quickly grow, make seeds, and die before the drought returns. Other plants have adapted to survive long periods without rain.

Finding Water

Most desert plants have extra-long roots to reach as much water as possible. Some roots spread out around the plants, forming tangled mats of thin roots that collect every drop of water. Other plants have really deep roots. For example, the roots of the mesquite reach up to 15 times as deep as the tree grows high. Fig trees in South Africa have the longest roots of all desert plants. They grow up to 330 feet (100 m) into the ground—as deep as a 30-story building is high!

Deep roots allow mesquite trees to grow well in places where drought is common.

Agaves store water in long, pointed leaves, while prickly pears have flattened, juicy stems.

Holding on to Water

To survive the drought, desert plants store water in their roots, stems, or leaves. Cacti have thick, fleshy stems filled with water, while aloe and agave have thick juicy leaves. Most plants lose a lot of water through their leaves, but desert plants have tough, narrow leaves that keep the water in. Cacti have spines instead of leaves. The sharp spines not only conserve water, but they also protect the plants from being eaten by thirsty animals.

Extreme!

Smart Drinker

The Namib Desert in southern Africa gets almost no rain, but the cold night air produces mist and drops of dew. Welwitschia is a strange-looking plant that has adapted to collect moisture from the air. The plant's two leaves split and curl so that drops of water run down the leaves straight to the plant's roots.

Chapter 3
At the Poles

The Arctic and Antarctica are Earth's coldest places, but the cold is not the only problem for wildlife. In winter, the sun never rises, making it dark all day long. In summer, the sun never sets. Some animals have adapted to live in these challenging habitats.

The Coldest Continent

Antarctica is permanently covered by ice up to nearly 3 miles (4.8 km) thick. Inland, the average temperature never climbs above freezing. In summer, it is about −4°F (−20°C), while in winter, it plummets to below −76°F (−60°C). Strong winds blow across the icy wasteland, making the air feel even colder. The mainland of Antarctica is too hostile for most wildlife. The Antarctic Peninsula and islands just outside the Antarctic zone are milder. The Southern Ocean that surrounds the continent is even warmer, so most Antarctic wildlife lives in the sea.

Antarctica is uninhabited by people except for visiting scientists. It is also too cold for most wildlife.

The Arctic

The tundra, the most northerly land in North America, Asia, and Europe, surrounds the Arctic Ocean. In the winter, the whole region is covered by ice. In summer, much of the ice melts. About three-quarters of the tundra is permafrost, which means that while the surface melts in summer, the ground below stays frozen. Animals in the Arctic have to overcome two severe problems—how to stop their bodies from freezing solid, and how to store up enough food to see them through the long, dark winter.

Reindeer lichen and other lichens and mosses carpet the tundra in summer.

Extra Extreme

When some deep ice melted in Alaska, scientists discovered bacteria that had been trapped in the ice for tens of thousands of years. Amazingly, as the bacteria thawed and warmed up, they came back to life and carried on as if they had never been frozen!

Keeping Warm

Many birds come to the tundra during the Arctic summer. They feed on mosses and lichens and produce young. When winter comes, they travel south to warmer climates. However, polar bears, Arctic foxes, seals, and other hardy mammals stay in the Arctic all winter. How do they keep warm?

Fat Suit

Seals, walruses, and polar bears have a thick layer of fat, called blubber, below their skin. Blubber insulates them when they swim in the freezing-cold water. A polar bear's favorite food is ringed seal, which it eats mainly for the blubber. The best time for polar bears to hunt is spring, when baby seals come onto the ice. Once the ice has melted, polar bears have to survive with little food until fall, when the ice freezes again.

Polar bears are so well insulated against the cold, they sleep on the ice.

Thick Fur

Arctic land mammals have thick fur all over their bodies. It traps air next to their skin. Air is a good insulator, so it keeps out the deadly cold. Polar bears and Arctic foxes even have thick fur under their feet. It insulates them against the ice and stops them from slipping. Many Arctic mammals have white fur to camouflage them against the white ice. Some animals that live on the tundra all year shed their white winter fur and grow brown fur for the summer.

Extreme!

Not Quite White

Polar bears look like they have white fur, but in fact their fur is transparent and hollow. It looks white because it reflects the light. The air inside the fur gives the bears extra insulation, especially when they swim in the freezing waters. Below the fur, their skin is black.

An Arctic fox's fur is white in winter but turns gray or brown in summer to blend in with the rocky tundra around it.

Natural Antifreeze

Antifreeze is a substance that stops water from freezing. Fish that live in the icy waters around Antarctica make their own antifreeze to stop their bodies from freezing solid. Several insects also make antifreeze to survive extremely cold Alaskan winters.

Ice Fish

Antarctic fish produce a special protein, which goes into action when ice crystals begin to form inside their bodies. The protein coats the crystals so that they cannot grow any bigger. The Southern Ocean around Antarctica is too cold for fish that live in warmer seas, so fish that make antifreeze have the waters to themselves. Arctic cod also produce an antifreeze protein, so fish at opposite ends of Earth have independently hit upon the same survival solution.

Around Antarctica ice floats in the ocean, which is warmer than the land but still freezing cold all year.

Supercooled Insects

In Alaska, snow fleas, yellow jackets, and stinkbugs can survive at temperatures as low as −13°F (−25°C). Without antifreeze proteins, these insects would freeze solid. Two types of beetles can supercool to below −100°F (−73°C). Red flat bark beetles spend the winter in damp spaces below the bark of balsam poplar trees. First they make antifreeze proteins, and then in late fall, they produce glycerol, a type of alcohol that slows down the formation of ice. Upis beetles use different tactics. They hide in dry places and allow their bodies to freeze, forcing water out of their cells as the temperature falls.

Extra Extreme

The red flat bark beetle is well prepared for the worst. It has survived temperatures much colder than any found in nature. In a lab in California, one of these beetles was cooled to −238°F (−150°C) and still survived!

23

Antarctic Wildlife

The Antarctic mainland is too cold for any amphibians, reptiles, or mammals to live. Birds, including skuas and albatrosses, visit nearby islands in spring and summer to lay eggs and raise their chicks. Most Antarctic animals, however, live in the cold waters around the continent. They include fish, squid, krill (a kind of shrimp), whales, dolphins, seals, and penguins. Penguins and seals spend part of their time ashore.

Mammals of the Sea

Many living things thrive in the Southern Ocean that surrounds Antarctica. The biggest are sea mammals, such as dolphins, seals, and sea lions, which have a thick layer of blubber to keep them warm in the icy seas. The blue whale, the largest animal that has ever lived, is at home there. It feeds on krill and masses of microscopic plants and animals, called plankton. Most sea mammals leave the Antarctic during the winter and swim to warmer seas to give birth to their young.

Antarctic fur seals come ashore to have pups in spring. Beaches may become crowded with penguins and other birds.

Suited for the Sea

Penguins cannot fly but are well adapted to spend most of their lives in the sea, where they feed on fish. They have webbed feet and use their wings as flippers to swim fast through the water. They are also well insulated, with a layer of blubber and many feathers, which trap warm air close to their skin and overlap tightly to make an oily, waterproof cover.

An emperor penguin chick relies on its parents and the warmth they give until it is old enough to reach the sea.

Extreme!

Patient Penguin

Male emperor penguins spend all winter standing on the Antarctic ice. Each one has an egg, which it keeps warm under a flap of skin. The penguin stops its feet from losing heat and freezing by reducing the amount of blood that reaches each foot.

Chapter 4

High Mountains

Nothing can live at the top of very high mountains because they are covered by ice all year round. A little farther down the mountainside, however, the ice melts in spring and summer, and hardy plants grow. They provide food and shelter for various mountain animals.

Hostile Conditions

The Himalayas are the world's highest mountain range. They include Mount Everest, the highest peak of all at 29,029 feet (8,848 m). The Andes in South America and the Rockies in North America are the longest ranges. High mountain slopes are blasted by strong winds, feel intensely cold, and have thin air, which gets thinner the higher you go. People who climb the highest mountains often carry tanks of oxygen to help them breathe. As the air thins, the temperature drops. It falls by about 10°F (6°C) for every increase in height of around 3,280 feet (1,000 m).

The Andean condor, one of the largest birds in the world, is a vulture and scavenger.

High Life

Only low-lying plants can grow on slopes up to the snow line, the height at which the permanent ice cap begins. Their roots dig into cracks in the rocks while the icy winds blow over them. High-living animals include small mammals, wild goats, birds of prey, and insects. At 22,000 feet (6,700 m), the Himalayan jumping spider is the highest resident. It feeds on frozen insects that have been carried up by the wind from below.

The peaks of the Himalayan mountains are one of the most extreme habitats on Earth.

Extra Extreme

The Himalayan jumping spider is a fierce hunter. It has eight eyes, including two extra-large eyes that act like binoculars. When the spider spots an insect, it jumps up to 30 times its own body length from rock to rock to reach prey.

Mountain Plants

Mountain plants need to be tough! They have to cope with bitter winds and freezing temperatures, thin soil, and hardly any water. The winters are long and cold, and the summers are short and chilly. Having survived the winter beneath the snow, plants have only a few months to flower and produce seeds.

Hugging the Ground

Most mountain plants have small, tough leaves and sturdy, woody stems. They protect themselves from the wind by growing close to the ground. Some plants form round cushions so that the wind blows over them. Others grow in sheltered cracks in the rocks. Mountain plants have long roots to take in extra water and to anchor themselves in the thin soil.

Alpine moss campion grows low to the ground, forms a cushion of plants, and flowers 2 to 6 inches (5 to 15 cm) high.

A giant lobelia's tall spike of flowers is covered with fluffy leaves, which insulate the tiny flowers during the freezing mountain nights.

Keeping Warm

Mountain plants have several ways of beating the cold. In winter, high mountain plants are covered by snow, which protects them from the icy winds. Some plants begin to grow even before the snow melts. Fine hairs that cover their leaves and stems insulate many plants from the cold. Giant lobelias, which grow high on Mount Kenya in Africa, have two ways of avoiding freezing. Long, feathery leaves insulate their small flowers, and their hollow stems contain a slightly sticky liquid that never freezes.

Extreme!

Head for Heights

Mountain buttercups grow higher up mountainsides than any other flower. They have bright-yellow petals to attract insects to pollinate their flowers and fertilize their seeds. However, the buttercups grow so high up, there are few insects to carry pollen from one flower to another. Luckily, they have a backup plan—unlike most flowers, they can pollinate themselves!

29

Mountain Animals

How do mountain animals withstand the long, cold winters and fierce winds? Some dig burrows like desert animals do and then go into a deep sleep, called hibernation. Others move farther down the mountain into the forests, where it is warmer. Finding food can be difficult all year round.

High Grazers

Mountain plants provide food for small mammals, such as marmets and chinchillas, and for wild sheep, goats, vicunas, and other larger animals. The plants are often scattered on steep slopes, so large mountain animals have to be nimble. Goats and sheep can climb and jump even when they are just a few hours old. Both animals have hooves that are split down the middle. Split hooves allow them to squeeze and grip the rocks with their feet.

A mountain goat with her two young kids make their way down a steep cliff.

Extreme!

Fast Food

Marmets spend most of the year hibernating in their burrows. When they wake up in May or June, they become extremely active. After their long sleep, they have just three months to feed, produce and raise young, and build up extra fat before they hibernate again.

Hunters and Scavengers

Grazing mammals are prey for snow leopards, mountain lions, and other predators. In North America, timber wolves hunt Dall sheep on the mountains of the Alaska Range, and lynx hunt birds and small mammals. Sheep and goats often escape by taking refuge on the steepest slopes. Eagles and condors soar high in the skies searching for prey on the slopes. Condors are scavengers that feed on dead animals. Live prey is scarce, so hunters, such as wolves and mountain cats, often scavenge as well as hunt.

A snow leopard stands on a high ridge and scans the slope for prey. She is well camouflaged, but so is her prey.

Chapter 5
Deep-Sea World

The most hostile region of the oceans is the deep sea, where it is always dark and the water is extremely cold. Also, the huge weight of seawater above creates enormous pressure, which would crush most animals to death. Humans need the protection of diving suits or special underwater craft to withstand the pressure. However, some extraordinary creatures live at the greatest depths of Earth's oceans.

Going Down

Light and warmth from the sun reach only the top 660 feet (200 m) of the ocean, called the sunlight zone, where most sea creatures live. Below that is the twilight zone, in which the water becomes increasingly cold and dark. Giant squid hide in the dim water and swim up toward the surface to hunt for food. The sperm whale does the opposite. It takes in a huge gulp of air at the surface and dives down to the twilight zone to hunt for giant squid, its favorite food.

A giant squid's long tentacles are lined with suckers for grasping prey.

Extra Extreme

Total Darkness

Even farther down is the totally dark midnight zone, which begins 3,280 feet (1,000 m) below the ocean surface. Strange fish and eels lurk there. At the very bottom of the ocean, the seabed forms a landscape of mountains, plains, and deep trenches. Most creatures that live on the ocean floor are invertebrates, meaning they have no backbones. They include sponges, brittle stars, shrimps, and tube worms. Even the deep trenches support some forms of life.

The deepest trench is the Mariana Trench off the coast of Japan. It plunges around 36,000 feet (10,970 m) below the ocean surface. The water above presses down with as much force as the weight of 48 Boeing 747 jumbo jets!

Tube worms grow around deep-sea vents, where nutrients seep up from below the ground. Squat lobsters and shrimps live there too.

Hunting in the Dark

Sea animals that live in the midnight zone prey on each other and scavenge what they can. However, there are few fish to hunt, and even these have to be found in pitch darkness. One meal may need to last a long time, so deep-sea animals have special adaptations to help them survive. Many have huge mouths and stretchy stomachs that allow them to swallow prey that is bigger than they are!

Making Light

Deep-sea fish often mix special chemicals in their bodies to produce their own light, called bioluminescence. Most of these fish produce blue-green lights because that color travels best through water. Some fish can flash their lights. The anglerfish uses its light to attract and trap prey. The light is at the end of a special fin that the fish dangles just above its mouth.

Only its green fluorescent lights reveal the shape of a shortnose greeneye fish.

This deep-sea fish is pink and red, colors that do not show up in the dark water. Its big eyes help it spot food among the corals.

Food from Above

Many deep-sea creatures are scavengers. The ocean floor receives a constant shower of dead fish and other sea animals that live in the sunlight and twilight zones. When any sea animal dies, its body eventually sinks to the bottom. A carcass soon attracts a mass of deep-sea scavengers. The first on the scene are usually small fish called macrourids. They swarm around any dead fish and devour it until it is all gone. The body of a large whale can supply food for millions of scavengers!

Extreme!

Seeing in the Dark

Fish called malacosteidae produce red lights, which act like night-vision devices. Most fish cannot see the color red, so malacosteidae use red lights to spot prey without being seen. They also produce blue-green lights, probably to warn other fish away.

Deepest of the Deep

The ocean floor is one of the least-explored biomes on Earth. Scientists once thought the ocean bed was mostly lifeless, but a team of international scientists working for the Census of Marine Life has discovered thousands of new kinds of bacteria and hundreds of previously unknown invertebrates, as well as some new species of fish.

Distant Habitat

Most of the ocean floor is a flat plain, called the abyssal plain. It is 10,000 to 20,000 feet (3,000 to 6,000 m) below the surface, at which point the water temperature is just above freezing. Inhabitants of the plain include invertebrates, such as worms and brittle stars, and fish, such as macrourids and tripod fish. Some spots on the abyssal plain are surprisingly hot. Water from hot underground rocks pours out at up to 750 °F (400 °C). Hot and cold vents provide minerals for microorganisms that feed soft corals, clams, large tube worms, and other invertebrates.

A brittle star is related to a starfish. It has five arms and can move fast across the sponges it lives on.

Extreme!

Making It Last

Amphipods are shrimplike creatures that live in all kinds of water. Hadal amphipods, though, live in the deepest parts of the ocean, in trenches up to 7 miles (11 km) below the surface. These amphipods feast on any remains that reach them. They can then survive for up to a year without food!

An amphipod is one of the most adaptable ocean species. It can even live in deep ocean trenches.

Low Life

In some places, deep ocean trenches break the abyssal plain. There are microorganisms and invertebrates there, but also one particular fish. The hadal snailfish lives 23,000 to 25,300 feet (7,000 to 7,700 m) below the surface of the ocean and is the deepest-living fish ever found. Its flesh is like jelly and it feeds by sucking up invertebrates.

Chapter 6
Burning Hot

Deserts are not the hottest habitats on Earth. Erupting volcanoes are too hot for any living things to survive in them, although hot volcanic springs do support microorganisms. Wildfires are common in many parts of the world. They destroy huge areas of plants and wildlife, but some animals have adapted to fire and even use it to their advantage.

Wild Wildfires

Wildfires occur when grasslands, the bush, or forests catch fire and the blaze spreads out of control. They are most common in places that are often hot, dry, and windy, such as the Southwest United States and Australia. With a strong wind, a fire can spread at a terrifying speed. The flames lick through dry grass and burn up leaves on trees and shrubs. The heat of the fire dries up the plants ahead of it, so they are quick to catch fire.

A wildfire can spread with terrifying speed through undergrowth and trees.

Escaping the Flames

Deer, bears, kangaroos, and other large animals run or hop as fast as they can to escape the flames. Old, sick, and young animals may not be fast enough, or their escape may be blocked by rivers or fences. Birds try to fly to safety before they are swept up in the flames. Small mammals, such as shrews and mice, burrow deeper into the ground to escape the heat. Snakes and lizards also burrow or shelter in cracks in rocks.

Extra Extreme

Fires often wipe out invertebrates, but some ants thrive on them. In the prairies of North America, there are usually more ants after a fire than there were before. The ants feast on the burned remains of dead animals!

Fire-Resistant Plants

Plants cannot escape from wildfires, but those that grow in habitats and biomes that experience many fires have developed different ways of surviving. Even if most of their stems and leaves are burned, many plants grow new shoots from roots and stems that have survived below the ground. Plants that do manage to survive the heat and flames can take advantage of the land freshly cleared by the fire.

Heat Treatment

Plants insulate themselves from fire in different ways. Some trees, such as ponderosa pines and giant sequoias, have extra-thick bark that does not burn through. Some protect their buds with clusters of needles or fire-resistant leaves. The eucalyptus tree has fire-resistant leaves—but it goes one step further. It produces resinous oils that burn easily, encouraging fires to destroy other plants and giving the eucalyptus more space for recovery.

Bluebush grows in Australia. It can survive a long-lasting fire and even the first flash of flames, provided the fire is not too hot.

Jack pine cones open and release their seeds only when their temperature reaches a burning 122°F (50°C).

Scattering Seeds

Some plants are so keen to take advantage of cleared land that they do not scatter their seeds until there is a fire. Pinecones contain pine seeds, which are scattered when the cones open. The cones of many types of pine trees, including the jack pine, open only after a fire. The cones of jack pines are held tightly shut by a sticky resin, which melts only at very high temperatures.

Extreme!

Waiting Game

What happens to jack pine seeds if there is no fire to open the cones? The answer is they wait. The seeds can be preserved for years inside the cones. Most cones open within six years, but even after 20 years about half the seeds in a jack pine cone are still able to grow.

In Hot Water

In some places on Earth, boiling-hot water bubbles out of the ground in hot springs or spurts out to form steaming geysers. Extremely hot rocks below the ground heat the water. This water is too hot for most forms of life, but not for heat-loving organisms called thermophiles.

Little Heat Seekers

Most plants and animals cannot live in water hotter than 104°F (40°C). Some insects can live in water up to 122°F (50°C), and some plants can even survive in water up to 140°F (60°C). Only thermophiles, such as cyanobacteria, also called blue-green algae, can live in even hotter water. Many hot pools are green because the blue-green algae that live there contain chlorophyll, the chemical needed for photosynthesis. However, chlorophyll cannot survive above 158°F (70°C), so thermophiles in extreme hot water live on minerals dissolved in the water and are often colorless.

Morning Glory Pool is a hot spring in Yellowstone National Park. Bacteria turn the pool green, blue, and yellow.

Blue-green algae clump together to form bright-orange mats around the edges of hot springs.

Hot Spring Food Chain

Thermophiles, particularly blue-green algae, can become the basis of food chains that support other animals, allowing them to live in or near hot springs. For example, blue-green algae thrive in hot springs in Yellowstone National Park. The algae provide food for the young larvae of the hot springs fly and other insects. In Africa, lesser flamingos live around hot salt lakes, where they feed on blue-green algae.

Extra Extreme

The champion thermophile is a microorganism called Strain 121. It lives around hot vents at the bottom of deep oceans and survives temperatures that are hotter than boiling water! Its name comes from the fact that it can survive at 250°F (121°C).

Chapter 7
Extraterrestrial Life

Scientists are amazed that microorganisms can live in the coldest, hottest, most hostile places on Earth. Are these microorganisms a clue to how life began on Earth? If life can survive in these places, could it also exist in other parts of our solar system?

Earliest Life on Earth

Some scientists think that life on Earth began around hot springs and deep-sea vents billions of years ago. Today, microorganisms that feed on minerals there become food for bacteria. More complex forms of life, such as tube worms, feed on the bacteria. Is this how life began and eventually evolved into all the different species that exist today?

Thick ice covers Jupiter's moon Europa, but scientists hope that the ocean below may support life.

Life Beyond Earth?

Space scientists are searching for signs of life on Mars and other planets and moons in the solar system. The first factor for life is water, and scientists know that water flowed on Mars in the past and that the chemicals necessary for life also exist there. They are looking for traces of microorganisms that existed in the past, or that might still live in the Martian soil. Both Jupiter and Saturn have moons of special interest to scientists. Europa, one of Jupiter's moons, is covered with a thick layer of ice, but from time to time, a fountain of water spurts 124 miles (200 km) into the sky. It must come from an ocean below the ice. Could microorganisms live in even this most hostile of homes?

Extreme!

Cosmic Creatures

Microscopic tardigrades, also known as water bears, are supreme survivors. They can survive extreme heat and cold and even intense radiation. They react to excessive cold by drying out completely, although scientists do not know how they do this. They have even survived in space!

The surface of the planet Mars is barren and hostile, but it may contain clues that life existed there in the past.

Glossary

abyssal plain a vast, flat plain at the bottom of the ocean

acid burning, sour-tasting substance

alkaline able to neutralize an acid

bacterium (plural bacteria) a tiny, single-celled living thing

bioluminescence light produced by living things

biome a large area with particular types of plants and climate

blubber a thick, tough fat layer found on sea mammals

camouflaged being colored or shaped to match the surroundings

carnivorous meat-eating

chlorophyll the green chemical in plants and some bacteria that takes in energy from sunlight

cyanobacteria bacteria that live in water and contain chlorophyll, which allows them to photosynthesize

drought a long time without rain

extremophiles living things that survive in extreme conditions

food chain the passing of energy from one living thing to another by eating and digesting

gills the body parts on an aquatic animal that extract oxygen dissolved in water

habitats the environments in which plants or animals live

hibernation a type of deep sleep used by animals to escape extreme conditions

insulate to protect from heat loss

invertebrates animals without spines or backbones

larvae (singular larva) the young stage of insects

microorganisms tiny living things

nutrients the substances that nourish living things

permafrost ground that is always frozen below the surface

photosynthesis to make sugar by combining water with carbon dioxide using sunlight

plankton microscopic plants and animals that drift in large masses in water

pollinate to carry pollen from one plant to another plant of the same type and allow it to produce seeds

protein a molecule that forms the substance of living things

radiation a form of energy that comes from the sun and some rocks

resinous made from a sticky substance produced by some plants and trees

scavengers animals that feed on the remains of dead animals and plants

species a type of living thing

thermophiles living things that can survive extreme heat

toxic poisonous

tundra a biome that has very cold conditions

For More Information

Books

Ganeri, Anita. *Harsh Habitats* (Extreme Nature). North Mankato, MN: Capstone, 2013.

Miller, Debbie S. *Survival at 120 Above*. New York, NY: Walker Childrens, 2012.

Owen, Ruth. *Arctic Foxes* (Polar Animals: Life in the Freezer). New York, NY: Rosen Publishing, 2013.

Simon, Seymour. *Seymour Simon's Extreme Earth Records*. San Francisco, CA: Chronicle Books, 2012.

Websites

Find out about polar bears and what they eat at:
kids.sandiegozoo.org/animals/mammals/polar-bear#animals

Discover why extremophiles are important at:
oceanservice.noaa.gov/facts/extremophile.html

See how birds and mammals that live in the desert have adapted to the extreme conditions at:
www.desertmuseum.org/books/nhsd_adaptations_birds.php

Understand photosynthesis and how plants get their nutrients at:
www.ncagr.gov/cyber/kidswrld/plant/nutrient.htm

Index